SAVING OUR PLANET

REUSE IT!

by
Mary Boone

PEBBLE
a capstone imprint

Pebble is published by Capstone,
1710 Roe Crest Drive, North Mankato, Minnesota 56003
www.capstonepub.com

**Library of Congress Cataloging-in-Publication Data is available on the
Library of Congress website.**
ISBN 978-1-9771-2580-4 (library binding)
ISBN 978-1-9771-2594-1 (paperback)
ISBN 978-1-9771-2600-9 (ebook pdf)

Summary:
Introduces early readers to environmentalist concepts including single-
use plastics and upcycling, and what they can do to help the environment.
Real-life examples of kids who have made a difference are featured.

Editorial Credits
Emily Raij, editor; Brann Garvey, designer; Svetlana Zhurkin,
media researcher; Katy LaVigne, production specialist

Image Credits
Newscom: Sipa USA/SOPA Images/Ana Fernandez, 13, SIPA/Schneider-
Press/W. Breiten, 20; Shutterstock: chaiyapruek youprasert, 12, chonticha
stocker, 6, DeawSS, 9, Elizaveta Galitckaia, 24, George Socka, 14,
HollyHarry, 27, Krzysztof Bargiel, 18, LightField Studios, 26, MIA Studio, 17,
Monkey Business Images, 19, myboys.me, 11, OAnderson, 25, overcrew,
7, SewCream, cover, TinnaPong, 5, 15, vystekimages, 29, Wassana
Panapute, 23

All internet sites appearing in back matter were available and accurate
when this book was sent to press.

TABLE OF CONTENTS

Words in **bold** are in the glossary.

SO MUCH GARBAGE

How much trash do you throw out a week? Now think about all the people who live around you. They throw out trash too. All that trash adds up.

Around the world, people throw away 2 billion tons of trash each year. That could fill 800,000 Olympic swimming pools. That's a lot of garbage!

Many **landfills** are full. When trash breaks down there, dirty gases go into the air. Some trash ends up in oceans or lakes. Wind or water can carry it there. This **pollution** kills birds, fish, and other animals. It also makes our drinking water dirty.

Making less trash can help. It's a first step toward solving these problems. Learn to reuse items. You'll throw away less trash. This protects the **environment**. Plus, it saves money.

Plastic causes some of the worst problems. Plastic water bottles, straws, forks, and spoons are everywhere. Plastic bags are too. Many of these are **single-use** plastics. They are used just one time. Then they are thrown away or recycled.

About 300 million tons of plastic are made each year. Plastic is useful. But about half is used just one time. That leaves a lot of trash.

BOTTLES, STRAWS, AND BAGS

Worldwide, people buy 1 million plastic bottles every minute. It takes a lot of **energy** to make them. They also cause pollution.

Want to limit how many plastic bottles you use? Use a water bottle you can refill over and over. This saves money. It also cuts down on bottles sent to the landfill or recycling center.

Lilly Platt is in elementary school. She is from the Netherlands. When Lilly was 7, she walked along the beach. She saw many plastic bottles washed up. It upset her. She wanted to help.

Two young people protesting pollution.

Now Lilly tells other kids about single-use plastics. Lilly picks up trash. She talks to lawmakers. She asks them to change laws to save the earth. Lilly is an **activist**.

Plastic straws are little. But they are a big problem. Most recycling centers won't take straws. Many straws that don't get thrown in the trash end up in oceans. More than 8 billion straws have washed up on beaches. Straws hurt wildlife. Some animals think straws look like food. They eat them. That makes them sick.

You can cut down on plastic trash. Skip the straw when you eat at restaurants. Metal, glass, bamboo, and hard plastic straws can be used over and over. Reusable straws are better for the earth.

Milo Cress lives in Vermont. When he was 7, he started thinking about plastic straws. He knew they caused problems. Milo started a project called Be Straw Free. He asked big companies to stop using plastic straws. Some of them listened.

Starbucks, McDonalds, and Alaska Airlines promised to stop using plastic straws. In 2018, Seattle became the first big U.S. city to ban plastic straws. Other cities are doing the same.

The average American family takes home 1,500 plastic shopping bags each year. Most don't get recycled. Many bags litter parks. They blow into lakes, rivers, and oceans. Each year, bags kill 100,000 **marine** animals. They eat or get tangled in the bags.

Reusable shopping bags limit trash.

Use the same bags each time you shop.

That saves animals and the planet.

Melati and Isabel Wijsen are sisters. They grew up on the island of Bali. They saw plastic bags littering their beaches. They decided to do something about it. They started a project called Bye Bye Plastic Bags.

The girls talked to lawmakers. They spoke about single-use plastic. The sisters taught others to use less plastic. They also talked about reusing.
In 2016, a law was passed to keep plastic bags out of Bali. Stores cannot use them. Bye Bye Plastic Bags is now a worldwide movement. They have cleanup teams in 25 cities.

Isabel (left) and Melati Wijsen
hold an award for their activism.

MORE WAYS TO REUSE

Reusable bottles, straws, and bags limit trash. But they are not the only things you can reuse. Look around your house. Search your recycling bins.

Are you throwing away things that could be reused? What items are you using just once? Can they be replaced with reusable things? Paper plates are one example. Those can't be recycled or reused. Use plates that can be washed. They are better for the planet.

23

Does your family buy items in glass jars? Instead of recycling the jars, clean them. Then reuse them. They can hold noodles or beans. Plant herbs in them. Store spices in small jars.

Jars can hold paper clips or rubber bands. They're great for storing nails and screws. You can use them as drinking glasses. How else could you reuse a jar?

Reusing gives things new life. Old T-shirts can become cleaning rags. Clothes that are too small can be worn by a younger sibling. They can be taken to a thrift store or given away too. When you finish a book, give it to a friend.

    Newspapers or old fabric can replace wrapping paper. Use egg cartons to sort craft supplies. Plastic butter tubs can store leftover food. Shop at thrift stores. If they have what you need, you will be reusing the items.

Reusing cuts down on trash. It helps the earth. It keeps animals safe. And it causes less pollution. You can start by cutting back on single-use plastics. Carry a refillable water bottle. Use your own shopping bags. Say no to plastic straws.

These small changes make a big difference. Soon, these changes will become habits. Your actions can help the world.

GLOSSARY

activist (AC-tiv-ist)—a person who works for social or political change

energy (E-nuhr-jee)—the ability to do work, such as moving things or giving heat or light

environment (in-VY-ruhn-muhnt)—all of the trees, plants, water, and dirt

landfill (LAND-fil)—a place where garbage is buried

marine (muh-REEN)—living in the sea

pollution (puh-LOO-shuhn)—materials that hurt Earth's water, air, and land

single-use (SING-guhl-yus)—something that can only be used one time

READ MORE

Ganeri, Anita. *Planet in Peril.* New York: Scholastic, 2019.

Lord, Michelle. *The Mess That We Made.* New York: Flashlight Press, 2020.

Whyman, Matt. *Our Planet: The One Place We All Call Home.* New York: HarperCollins Children's Books, 2019.

INTERNET SITES

Bye Bye Plastic Bags
byebyeplasticbags.org

Eco-Cycle Be Straw Free Campaign
ecocycle.org/bestrawfree

The Kid Should See This: How Trash Is Recycled
thekidshouldseethis.com/post/recycle-video-for-kids

INDEX